Contents

CW00486743

3

What's Special about Open Countryside?

A few remote mountain areas of Wales - notably in Snowdonia, the Cambrians and the Brecon Beacons – are almost the only inland relics of natural habitats dating from before the ascent of Man. Before the Stone Age, what we now see as moorland and heath was woodland (the 'wildwood') rich in elm, lime and oak trees that had covered most of the UK since the end of the last ice age. Until about 2000 BC, therefore, most of the floral diversity of Wales was confined to the coastal strip, riversides and lake margins.

As early livestock farmers created forest clearings and light fell on the bare earth, wildflower seeds, blown in or carried by birds and mammals, colonised the land. The most productive open areas were cultivated, and as exotic grain and vegetable species were brought in from overseas so more non-native wildflowers – poppies for example – became part of the country scene. Neglected acid flat land, lightly grazed by sheep and extensively tunnelled by rabbits and other small mammals, soon turned to lowland heath or upland moors dominated by ling and heather (left) with relatively few other flower species. When myxomatosis killed most of the rabbits and reduced the natural cultivation even fewer seeds could germinate, and shrubs encroached on the heath.

Today some of our rarest wildflower species teeter on the brink of extinction, holding out on a mere handful of inaccessible ledges and peat bogs where the sheep cannot cut them down. Too many sheep and the heath and moors would turn to dust or mire; too few and scrub, birch and eventually hardwood forest would eventually blanket the land.

Just as the future biodiversity of our mountain, moorland and heath habitats requires a sustainable, eco-friendly livestock farming regime so also the wildflowers of lowland permanent pasture and crop fields are at the mercy of arable farming. Sparing field margins from fertilisers, insecticides and herbicides not only provides habitats for wild animals and insects for birds and amphibians; it also ensures that future generations will be able to enjoy the diversity of wildflowers that, enigmatically, farming itself has produced.

4

Meadows – an ever-changing landscape

An initial effect of arable farming on the wildflowers of our lowland countryside must have been to spread them more widely. As crops were taken to market so also were 'weed' seeds transported from one part of the country to another. This increased the diversity of wildflowers that could be seen at one locality, but sometimes they smothered rarer plants.

Gardeners also affected wildflower distributions and abundance, and not just by letting exotic invasive plants escape into the wild. It's hard to imagine that people who so obviously loved flowers would scour the countryside for plants to fill their gardens, but these plant collectors – some making it a full-time business – brought many of our rarest and most beautiful wildflowers to the verge of extinction. When chemical cleaning of agricultural seeds and the widespread use of herbicides and fertiliser became the norm, even some formerly common species virtually (or actually) disappeared from the Welsh landscape.

Field cow-wheat, *Melampyrum arvensis* (right), no longer grows along the Wales-England border – indeed, it is now extremely rare in the UK, being confined to a few small sites on chalk downland.

Corn cockle, *Agrostemma githago* (below, right), was once a common cornfield flower. For all practical purposes it is now extinct in the wild, although some wildflower meadow mixtures' include it.

Many other wildflowers, including thorow-wax, downy hemp-nettle and violet horned-poppy, are already extinct, their places on the Red Data Book list of rare and endangered species quickly taken up by other victims of the side-effects of our unsustainable lifestyles.

UK Biodiversity Action Plan (UKBAP)

The desperate plight of wildflowers of arable land and field margin habitats has now been formally recognised in the UK Biodiversity Action Plan, where species in need of conservation action are listed and action plans have been drawn up to try to ensure their survival. More than 60 rare or scarce flowering plants are listed, several of which are wildflowers of arable land. But even with the help of volunteer labour, conservation work costs money. The work will go on provided that future generations choose to continue investing in the protection of wildlife and floral biodiversity. If only they would care to learn, we are sure they would learn to care.

Snowdon Lily *(Lloydia serotina)*

© 2006 Dr Barbara Jones

The Snowdon lily, with its solitary bell-shaped flower, is one of Wales's rarest wildflowers. Nowadays it is seldom seen anywhere but in the most inaccessible rock ledges and crevices. Confined to just a few locations in Snowdonia, it was discovered there in the late 17th century by Edward Llwyd. The flower, named after its discoverer (unusually, this happened during his lifetime) is also known locally as 'y bryfedlog', meaning spiderwort – a reference to the spidery appearance of the Snowdon lily's slender leaves.

This arctic-alpine plant grows in Wales, and close relatives occur in mountainous areas of mainland northern Europe; however, rather surprisingly, it has not been found in Scotland

Jan   Feb   Mar   Apr   May   Jun   Jul   Aug   Sep   Oct   Nov   D

Fritillary *(Fritillaria meleagris)*

This lovely wildflower inhabits damp meadows. Its solitary bell-shaped blooms, which can vary in colour from purple to creamy-white, have an almost chequered appearance.

< 30mm >

Although occasional colonies of wild fritillaries can still be found in the Welsh Marches, notably along the border with Shropshire, this distinctive member of the lily family, Liliaceae, is in serious decline as a result of field drainage, ploughing of pastureland and the application of fertilisers. In other parts of Wales naturalised fritillaries can still be seen in managed damp grassland and beside streams in parks.

The flowers are hermaphrodite (having both male and female parts) and so the plant is self-fertile.

As with so many other kinds of lilies the bulb is poisonous, but the plant itself has been used in the past as a healing herb.

Globe Flower *(Trollius europaeus)*

Around each flower ten or more yellow sepals curve inwards to form a globe – hence the common name of this impressive member of the buttercup family (Ranunculaceae).

< **40mm** >

The globe flower favours damp meadows and ditches in hilly countryside, and so it is widely distributed across upland Wales. Good places to see globe flowers include Snowdonia National Park and Cwm Cadlan on the southern fringe of the Brecon Beacons National Park. In Powys there are plenty of damp meadows where the globe flower and numerous other heath and moorland species, including orchids, can be found.

At Dolfrwynog Bog, north of Dolgellau, site of the former Turf Copper Mine, the peaty soil now contains high concentrations of copper-bearing chemicals that many wildflowers cannot tolerate. Globe flower, being one of the relatively few plants that can cope with copper pollution, actually thrives there.

Jan   Feb   Mar   Apr   May   Jun   Jul   Aug   Sep   Oct   Nov   D

ommon Cotton-grass *(Eriophorum angustifolium)*

ith their flowing cotton-like hairs, the fleecy seed heads of common cotton-grass wave
d bob in the summer breeze. Wherever this plant is abundant it appears almost as
ough a snowstorm has turned the landscape brilliant white.

In April and May the flowers, much less significant than the seed heads, are borne on stems that are three-sided at the top.

The alternative common name bog cotton gives a clue to the habitat needs of this plant.

Where it occurs beside moorland streams, cotton-grass is the preferred food of the (increasingly rare) water vole.

< 50mm >

Bog Asphodel *(Narthecium ossifragum)*

< 14mm >

Bog asphodel thrives on the wet peaty heaths and moors of Wales. It is prolific in the bog moorland areas of the Hafren Forest, in mid Wales, where the River Severn (Afon Hafren) rises. Once the star-like flowers have died, the fruiting stems turn bright orange.

Jan   Feb   Mar   Apr   May   Jun   Jul   Aug   Sep   Oct   Nov   D

Corn Marigold *(Chrysanthemum segetum)*

Before the introduction of modern weedkillers, farmers regarded the corn marigold as a serious pest and they employed women to work in the fields pulling up the plants.

< 55mm >

Mainly seen nowadays as a garden escape, the wild corn marigold is in serious decline but still occurs in some arable field margins.

Not merely tolerating but apparently favouring acid soils, this lovely member of the daisy family (Asteraceae) was once very common in Wales - indeed, the English meaning of the name of the mid-Wales village of Llandeilo Graban is St Teilo's Church of the Corn Marigold.

Cornflower *(Centaurea cyanus)*

< 25mm >

The cornflower is another wildflower that grain producers once regarded as a troublesom weed and worked hard to eradicate, although anyone who has seen a sunlit field of golde corn rippled with swathes of blue cannot fail to be impressed by its beauty.

Cornflowers sometimes reappea when the soil around field margi is disturbed after long periods o being untouched.

Listed as a nationally endangere species throughout England and Wales, most large patches of cornflowers seen in Wales toda almost certainly originated from wildflower seed mixtures; withou regular replanting such colonies seldom last for many years.

Jan   Feb   Mar   Apr   May   Jun   Jul   Aug   Sep   Oct   Nov   D

Carline Thistle *(Carlina vulgaris)*

Quite different from any other thistle, this plant has been used as a herbal purgative. It is still common in Wales, particularly on short, dry grassland on calcareous soil.

The carline thistle is much more conspicuous during the winter months, when it doesn't have to compete for our attention with more colourful wildflowers. The seed heads are almost identical to its inconspicuous brownish-yellow flowers.

Sometimes referred to as weather thistles, the flower heads expand during dry spells and close in humid weather. Once dried, the flowers continue to open and close in this way for several months, so acting as a simple hygrometer for use in weather forecasting.

Jan   Feb   Mar   Apr   May   Jun   Jul   Aug   Sep   Oct   Nov   Dec   *13*

Common Rock-rose *(Helianthemum nummularium)*

Although found throughout Wales, common rock-rose (not a rose at all but a member of t
family Cistaceae) prefers chalk and limestone grassland. It is particularly abundant on the
Great Orme, near Llandudno, and at Kenfig National Nature Reserve, near Bridgend.

< 22mm >

The colour of the pretty flowers
on this creeping, evergreen shru
varies from white through yellow
to orange.

Although it produces neither
scent nor nectar, the rock-rose
visited by insects for its pollen. A
a result some of the pollen is
transferred to other rock-rose
flowers nearby. This versatile litt
wildflower is also capable of
asexual reproduction, and wher
the flowers close in dull or wet
weather the petals push the
pollen-laden stamens against th
female styles.

Dandelion *(Taraxacum officinale)*

Common they may be, but few floral sights can rival dandelions as they smother a field or a patch of wasteland on a bright spring day. The general term dandelion is applied to some 250 short perennial plants, the most common being the group known as Ruderalia.

The dandelion is characterised by leafless hollow stems that exude a milky juice when picked. The seed head is equally well-known and loved as the 'dandelion clock' – the number of blows required to remove all the seeds tells the hour of the day.

Dandelion is also known as 'wet-the-bed' and not without reason – it has long been used as a diuretic and laxative. The leaves are still used in salads today, and some consider their flavour to be better than that of the forced lettuces that are all that many shops can offer us in the winter months. Dandelion wine remains popular, and there are many local recipes for making it.

Common Daisy *(Bellis perennis)*

>18mm<

The common daisy is a member of our largest family of flowering plants, the Asteraceae (also known as the composites). Most children play at making daisy chains, but in Wales there is also a tradition of making daisy caterpillars; this involves threading lots of daisy heads on to one flower with a long stem. Some of the sandy golf links in Wales have such dense carpets of daisies (which quickly reappear after close mowing) that it is almost impossible to see where a golf ball lands on the fairways.

Mountain Avens *(Dryas octopetala)*

This beautiful wildflower likes short limey turf and can be found on mountain ledges in Snowdonia. Although rare, it has survived in Wales since the end of the last ice age.

< 30mm >

Resembling anemones, the flowers of mountain avens have brilliant white petals and a mass of bright yellow stamens. After flowering, the twisted and feathery seed-heads appear (inset left).

The specific name *ocotopetala* suggests that the flower has eight petals; however, as with the unusual specimen shown on the left, occasionally you can come across flowers with as many as ten or even a dozen petals.

Tansy *(Tenacetum vulgare)*

< 9mm >

Favouring dry, sunny grassland and wasteland sites, tansy can be found from Conwy in th north to Cardiff in the south, but this wildflower is rarely abundant anywhere in Wales.

A member of the daisy family, Asteraceae, tansy is a strongly aromatic perennial. The leaves which taste peppery, were use in Tansy Cake, a traditional Easter fare in times gone by. Even today some people brew tansy-leaf tea, although in large doses it can be a violent irritant and in the USA it has been linked to several deaths. For the victims the generic name *Tanacetum*, derived from the Greek word for immortality, wa surely inappropriate.

The tansy beetle, *Chrysolina graminis*, relies on this plant fo food, as also did the Essex emerald moth, *Thetidia smaragdaria maritima*, which has now been officially declare as extinct in the UK.

Meadow Buttercup *(Ranunculus acris)*

A sunlit meadow swathed in these tall and graceful wildflowers - surely the best known and loved of all our buttercups – must rank as one of the finest sights of our countryside.

< 20mm >

The children's game of holding a glossy buttercup flower under the chin is still popular today. If the skin reflects a yellow glow, it signifies that they like butter. (The answer is always a foregone conclusion, of course.)

The name buttercup only became common in the eighteenth century; before that time these flowers were known by a host of other local, common names such as goldweed and kingcups - the latter being a name now most often given to marsh marigolds, *Caltha palustris.*

Jan   Feb   Mar   Apr   May   Jun   Jul   Aug   Sep   Oct   Nov   Dec   *19*

Meadow Cranesbill *(Geranium pratense)*

Meadow cranesbill is a large plant with flowers ranging from violet-blue to a soft purple.

< 30mm >

This once very common wildflower favours lime-rich grassland and damp meadows, but numerous cultivars and hybrids escape from gardens and are frequently to be seen on roadside verges.

The cranesbills are so called because the fruiting head that follows the flower ends in a long pointed 'beak' like that of the crane, a large bird with a very long beak. (The family name *Geranium* comes from *Geranos*, the classical Greek word meaning a crane.)

Common Poppy *(Papaver rhoeas)*

Before the use of chemical sprays became so prevalent, the common poppy could often be seen reddening the fields of arable crops. Today, this beautiful wildflower is mainly confined to the edges of fields and to ground that has been recently disturbed.

80mm

Poppies have spread so successfully that they now occur almost everywhere on the planet where arable crops are grown. How and when they reached Wales is unclear, however, and the seeds may even have been brought in to Britain by Neolithic settlers.

Red poppies have long been associated with fertility but also with death. Today this flower is probably best known as the emblem of Remembrance Day, when we pay tribute to those who died during the two World Wars. (Wild red poppies quickly colonised the disturbed fields of battle.)

Mountain Everlasting *(Antennaria dioica)*

Mountain everlasting, a member of the daisy family, Asteraceae, can be found on dry heath and mountain slopes throughout Wales. This unusual plant has male (pictured above) and female flowers (below) that differ markedly. The specific name *dioica* is of Greek origin and means 'two houses' – a reference to the separate male and female plants.

< 40mm >

Being a perennial plant, mountain everlasting springs up in the same place year after year, which may be the origin of its common name. Another possible explanation is that in the past, when this plant was much more plentiful, the flowers were gathered and dried to provide indoor floral displays through the winter.

Jan Feb Mar Apr May Jun Jul Aug Sep Oct Nov De

Heather *(Calluna vulgaris)*

< 4mm >

In autumn great tracts of the Welsh moorland and mountain landscape turn purple when heather, our most abundant member of the heath family, Ericaceae, comes into bloom. The so-called 'lucky white heather' is far less common than the pink-purple variety.

Heather, also known as ling, has long been a valued source of food, fuel and building material. The honey-scented flowers made it a popular bedding material and were also the source of an orange dye; they were even used to make beer.

During the 2001 foot-and-mouth disease outbreak a Clwyd brick maker used heather as packing material for bricks sent to Ireland when using straw (the usual packing material) was not permitted.

Bell Heather *(Erica cinerea)*

Bell heather has flowers much brighter and slightly larger than those of heather and it starts blooming earlier, continuing to produce flowers throughout summer and autumn.

> 6mm <

Whereas common heather can cope with a wide range of ground conditions, bell heather favours drier heaths and moors. In boggy areas bell heather and common heather often grow together, with the bell heather commanding the high spots as though they were stepping stones Crossing open moorland can be very risky, but a trail of bell heather clumps can serve to mark a less hazardous route.

Cross-leaved Heath *(Erica tetralix)*

< 8mm >

Rather than bearing spikes of flowers, as heather and bell heather do, this member of the heath family (Ericaceae) has heads of typically eight or ten rose pink bell-shaped flowers.

A close look at the leaves helps to distinguish bell heather and cross-leaved heath. All the way up the flowering stems of bell heather (shown left) there are side shoots that look like bunches of leaves. Cross-leaved heath has whorls of four leaves (the origin of its specific name *tetralix*) spaced up the woody stems.

Unlike bell heather, cross-leaved heath favours wet habitats and can be found in bogs, wet heaths and moors throughout Wales.

Jan   Feb   Mar   Apr   May   Jun   Jul   Aug   Sep   Oct   Nov   Dec   *25*

Bilberry *(Vaccinium myrtillus)*

Also known as whortleberry, wimberry or huckleberry, our bilberry is a smaller version of its American counterpart the blueberry. The blue-black berries (insert, above) are delicious.

< 5mm >

In autumn ripe bilberries can be picked to make jam or for drying to use as currants. In the past a blue-black dye was made from the fruits and a dark green dye from the leaves of this member of the heath family (Ericaceae).

The berries tend to hide beneath the dark-green leaves, and so a coarse-toothed metal comb is considered the most effective tool for stripping bilberries from the plants.

In Wales bilberry picking was once a significant industry, particularly in parts of Gwent and the Vale of Clywd.

Pineappleweed *(Matricaria discoidea)*

> 8mm <

An introduced annual weed causing problems for growers of intensive vegetable crops, but also found on wasteland and beside paths through permanent pastures, this perennial plant is very common throughout Wales. Also known as pineapple mayweed, this rayless member of the daisy family, Asteraceae, was introduced into the UK in 1821 and quickly spread along roadsides, carried with mud on cartwheels and, later, vehicle tyres.

Pineappleweed has several medical uses, including as a worming treatment. As its common name suggests, the crushed flower heads smell of pineapple.

< 20mm >

Another member of the daisy family, **feverfew (Tanacetum parthenium)** has a shorter flowering season than pineapple mayweed. Almost certainly brought to Britain for medicinal uses, feverfew was indeed thought to be a cure for fever and headaches. The specific name comes from the Greek word *parthenos*, a maiden – thought by some to be a reference to its reputed ability to strengthen the womb.

The masses of flowers can be seen from June to September in field margins and on wasteland throughout Wales but most commonly close to habitation.

an   Feb   Mar   Apr   May   Jun   Jul   Aug   Sep   Oct   Nov   Dec

Yellow Rattle *(Rhinanthus minor)*

< 15mm >

For those seeking wild orchids, the sight of yellow rattle creates a sense of expectation, because orchids and yellow rattle are often found in the same habitats.

The generic name *Rhinanthus* comes from the Greek words for nose and flower, a fanciful reference to a fairytale witch's hooked nose suggested by the petals of yellow rattle. Even more obviously, the common name comes from the ripe fruit (see left) rattling around inside the enlarged sepals that remain joined after the flowers have died back.

This hemi-parasitic plant of calcareous lowland hay meadows and heath attaches its roots to those of grasses and draws water and nutrients from them, apparently without too serious an effect on the host plant. Also sometimes referred to as hay rattle, where it grows in abundance this wildflower can turn the landscape a deep golden yellow.

Yellow rattle, which occurs throughout Wales, is a member of the figwort family, Scrophulariaceae.

Jan   Feb   Mar   Apr   May   Jun   Jul   Aug   Sep   Oct   Nov   De

Heath Spotted Orchid *(Dactylorhiza maculata)*

< 10mm >

This orchid's similarity to the common spotted orchid, with which it frequently hybridises, makes the already difficult job of distinguishing the two species almost impossible for anyone but a real orchid expert. The flowers of the heath spotted orchid tend to be borne in rather flatter, shallower spikes than those of the common spotted orchid. The lower lip of the flower has but a short central tooth rather than being deeply lobed. Perhaps the best clue to identity is that heath spotted orchids have narrow leaves and favour acid soil while common spotted orchids have broader leaves and prefer limey soil. Good places for heath spotted orchids in mid Wales include the Elan Estate and the Lake Vyrnwy Nature Reserve.

Jan   Feb   Mar   Apr   May   Jun   Jul   Aug   Sep   Oct   Nov   Dec   *29*

Sneezewort *(Achilea ptarmica)*

< 15mm >

Sneezewort, a member of the daisy family, Asteraceae, is found in all parts of Wales. It prefers acid soil and can be found in damp grassland and acid heath habitats.

The specific name *ptarmica* comes from the Greek word *ptarmes,* means sneezing. Like the English common name, it is a reference to the ability of sneezewort to clear nasal passages when its pollen is sniffed. This was not the only virtue ascribed to sneezewort, however: in the Middle Ages, toothache sufferers would chew its acrid roots to deaden the pain.

The composite flower consists of many tiny florets. The 8 to 18 white rays are outer petals of edge florets, each of which has one large petal, the others being tiny like those of the regular inner florets.

Yarrow *(Achillea millefolium)*

< 5mm >

Yarrow is a strongly aromatic perennial plant with white or occasionally pink-purple flowers. This member of the daisy family (Asteraceae) is found in grassy habitats throughout Wales.

Like its close relative sneezewort, yarrow has (usually five) white rays formed by the outer florets each bearing one enlarged petal. Very dark pink specimens found in the wild are nearly always the result of cross-pollination with garden varieties of yarrow.

Legend has it that the Greek warrior Achilles used yarrow to cure arrow wounds – hence the generic name. The specific name *millefolium* means a thousand leaves and is a reference to the very finely divided grey-green leaves of this common wildflower.

Yarrow is also known as poor man's pepper and as staunchweed - the latter referring to its use to treat open wounds, although we now know that it can cause allergic skin rashes.

Greater Knapweed *(Centaurea scabiosa)*

40mm

Greater knapweed grows in meadows mainly in limestone areas and always has rayed petals. Flowers of **common knapweed (*Centaurea nigra*)**, also known as hardheads, are smaller and can occur in either rayed form or, as the sample inset above, without rays.

The heads of common knapweed are covered by overlapping dark brown bracts and can appear almost black, while those of greater knapweed retain a greener tinge. This distinctive feature is mainly due to the shape of the feathery tips of the bracts: those of greater knapweed (left) have horseshoe-shaped dark appendages while in common knapweed they are round or triangular and overlap so that very little of the green area shows.

The knapweeds are members of the daisy family (Asteraceae).

Lousewort *(Pedicularis sylvatica)*

Lousewort is a hemi-parasitic plant often found on acid grassland, especially on damp moors and heaths. This low-growing wildflower is common throughout Wales.

There is no real evidence that lousewort can spread lice, but an association with lice infestation of grazing animals is implied in both the common name and the scientific name of this plant. (*Pedis* is the Latin for louse.)

The two-lipped flowers are usually pale pink, but sometimes (as in the example pictured left) they are pure white.

Lousewort belongs to the figwort family, Scrophulariaceae.

Fragrant Orchid *(Gymnadenia conopsea)*

< 12mm >

This pale pink to purple (occasionally white) flowers of this lovely orchid are, as its name suggests, strongly scented especially in the evening. Fragrant orchids can be found throughout Wales; in most years they bloom prolifically on the Elan Estate in Powys.

34   Jan   Feb   Mar   Apr   May   Jun   Jul   Aug   Sep   Oct   Nov   Dec

Hoary Plantain *(Plantago media)*

18mm

Most plantains have drab flowers, but the fuzzy pink stamens give this grassland species a lovely halo. Hoary plantain can be found in most limestone regions, and it is particularly plentiful in Denbighshire, south Pembrokeshire and the Brecon Beacons area. Unusually for a member of the family Plantaginaceae it is scented and so bees pollinate it.

Jan   Feb   Mar   Apr   May   Jun   Jul   Aug   Sep   Oct   Nov   Dec   *35*

Self-heal *(Prunella vulgaris)*

Much visited by bumblebees and many other insects, the flowers of self-heal can tolerate frequent cutting and so can be seen blooming through spring, summer and autumn.

< 40mm >

Common in permanent pastures and heathland, this member of the mint family, Lamiaceae, is also often seen in lawns. Self-heal adapts its height to the length of the grass in which it grows, and so although usually a very short plant it can grow up to 30cm tall.

Self-heal has a long history as a treatment for wounds, cuts, bruises, sores and ulcers. Its culinary uses include salads, stews, casseroles and soups, and a drink can be made from the leaves.

Jan   Feb   Mar   Apr   May   Jun   Jul   Aug   Sep   Oct   Nov   Dec

Frog Orchid *(Dactylorhiza viridis)*

< 7mm >

The diminutive frog orchid can be very difficult to spot, but once your eye has become tuned in to its unique flower shape it is possible to find some really good specimens. This neat little orchid favours lime-based short grassland in a number of habitats including meadows, dunes and even high rocky ledges.

Nowhere in the UK can the frog orchid be truly described as abundant, but one of its strongholds is the limestone pastures of north-east Wales. There are also records of this species appearing in small numbers in Anglesey, Snowdonia and Pembrokeshire as well as on the South Wales coastal strip and along the Wales-England border.

When looking at the flower of this inconspicuous orchid try thinking of a jumping frog and maybe, just maybe, it will remind you of one.

Jan   Feb   Mar   Apr   May   Jun   Jul   Aug   Sep   Oct   Nov   Dec   *37*

Germander Speedwell *(Veronica chamaedrys)*

< 10mm >

A sprawling perennial plant with white-centred azure blue flowers, germander speedwell is very common in Welsh meadows and churchyards and in many other grassy places.

Some say that the name speedwell refers to various rapid-healing properties; others link it to the fact that the petals fall very soon after the flowers are picked. The phrase 'speed well' meaning 'safe journey' was also used as an alternative to goodbye.

There was a time when tea made from the dried leaves of germander speedwell was thought to cure gout.

This and the many other speedwell species are all members of the figwort family, Scrophulariaceae.

Heath Speedwell *(Veronica officinalis)*

More compact than germander speedwell and with spikes of flowers less blue and more lilac or occasionally purple, heath speedwell favours uncultivated acid grassland.

Also referred to sometimes as common speedwell – despite the fact that many of the other 20 or so speedwells found in the British Isles occur far more commonly than heath speedwell – the specific name *officinalis* indicates that the plant was considered to have medicinal properties.

The generic name may be a dedication to St Veronica, a woman of Jerusalem who according to legend (not the Bible) offered Jesus a handkerchief with which to wipe his face before he took up the cross on the road to Calvary. The story says that the 'Veil of Veronica' was left bearing a picture of the face of Jesus and that Veronica later travelled to Rome, where she presented the veil to the Roman Emperor Tiberius. By the Middle Ages the veil was widely considered to bear the true image of Jesus Christ.

The name *Veronica* comes from the Latin *vera*, meaning true, and the Greek *icon*, meaning image.

Common Ragwort *(Senecio jacobaea)*

A field aglow with golden ragwort is an impressive sight, but because of the liver damage it causes when eaten by horses or cattle it is one of the most persecuted of weeds. Ragwort causes about half of all cases of poisoning of farm livestock in the UK.

18mm

Serious problems can occur if this plant is inadvertently included in hay that is fed to horses or cattle. Sheep, on the other hand, seem to be unaffected by the alkaloid poison in ragwort, at least when they eat it in small amounts.

As with dandelions, the seeds of ragwort are attached to hairy parachutes that are spread widely by the breeze. Under the Control of Weeds Act, if the seeds are likely to spread to nearby grazing land then a landowner is required to remove and destroy ragwort plants before they are able to flower.

A member of the daisy family, Asteraceae, ragwort is the staple diet of the caterpillar (pictured left) of the cinnabar moth, *Tyria jacobaeae*, which feeds on its leaves.

Jan   Feb   Mar   Apr   May   Jun   Jul   Aug   Sep   Oct   Nov   Dec

Field Scabious *(Knautia arvensis)*

30mm

This lovely nodding wildflower is a member of the teasel family, Dipsacaceae. It is found in dry pastures and along the edges of cultivated fields, mainly on calcareous soil.

The generic name *Knautia* is a reference to the 17th century German botanist Christopher Knaut, while the specific name *scabious* comes from the plant's former use as a treatment for scabies, a skin complaint that results in scabs.

Field scabious is also known locally as lady's pincushion and as blue bonnets.

Jan   Feb   Mar   Apr   May   Jun   Jul   Aug   Sep   Oct   Nov   Dec   *41*

Greater Butterfly Orchid *(Platanthera chlorantha)*

22mm

The brilliant, almost phosphorescent flowers of the greater butterfly orchid are very easy to spot from a distance, even in the poor light of evening.

This relatively loose-flowered orchid occurs most commonly on lime-based grassland and occasionally on the edges of woods. The name butterfly orchid is not, as some might mistakenly assume, a reference to its pollination by butterflies but rather to the shape of the flower. The greenish-white, somewhat translucent flowers are known to be pollinated by moths that are attracted by the light vanilla scent.

The long spur of this orchid is both a source of nectar and a cunning means of ensuring pollination. The sweet liquid fills only the bottom half of the spur tube, and so a moth has to get up close to push its tongue deep enough into the tube to secure nectar. In so doing the insect brushes its head against the pollinia – a pair of short pollen-bearing stamens that are situated on either side of the tube opening. Pollen attached to the moth's head is then carried to another greater butterfly orchid flower, where it comes into contact with the stigma. By this process cross-pollination is achieved.

Greater butterfly orchids are found in grassland throughout Wales. A very good place to see them is Caeau Tan y Bwlch, a nature reserve on the Lleyn Peninsula managed by North Wales Wildlife Trust on behalf of Plantlife.

42   Jan   Feb   Mar   Apr   May   Jun   Jul   Aug   Sep   Oct   Nov   Dec

Lesser Butterfly Orchid *(Platanthera bifolia)*

The lesser butterfly orchid is very similar to but usually smaller overall than its relative the greater butterfly orchid. The flowers have longer spurs and are also rather greener.

The best way to be certain of the identity of a butterfly orchid is to examine the pollinia. In the lesser butterfly orchid these pollen-bearing stamens are in the form of a narrow parallel column, whereas the pollinia of the greater butterfly orchid are more widely spaced and the gap between them tapers so that the columns are further apart at their bases than they are at their tips.

More frequent on the western side of Wales, the lesser butterfly orchid occurs mainly on moorland and in bogs, although it can sometimes be found in damp permanent pastures.

The Latin species name *bifolia* refers to the two large basal leaves; indeed, before the flowers develop it is very easy to mistake lesser butterfly orchids for twayblades.

There are lesser butterfly orchids at North Wales Wildlife Trust's Cors Goch reserve, on Anglesey. There the limestone grassland is home to green-winged orchids and fragrant orchids (see page 34) with the lesser butterfly orchid occurring in the low-lying damp areas.

In Carmarthenshire, Plantlife's nature reserve at Cae Blaen-dyffryn comprises just a single meadow. There, in June, both lesser and greater butterfly orchids bloom along with a wonderful display of ragged robin and many other grassland and marsh plants. In recent years more than 5000 butterfly orchid plants have been recorded in this small reserve.

20mm

| Jan | Feb | Mar | Apr | May | Jun | Jul | Aug | Sep | Oct | Nov | Dec |

Sainfoin *(Onobrychis viciifolia)*

An import from mainland Europe, sainfoin was cultivated in Wales and throughout the UK for several centuries and was used as a fodder crop for cattle. It is now seen very rarely.

50mm

The common name comes from the French *sain foin*, meaning wholesome hay. Although grown primarily in the belief that it would increase milk yield of dairy cattle, sainfoin was also thought to have other useful properties. The leaves were used to make poultices for drawing out boils, and sainfoin was also fed to people suffering from certain painful bladder disorders.

Chalk and limestone grassland are the preferred habitats of this spectacularly beautiful member of the pea family, Fabaceae.

Bush Vetch *(Vicia sepium)*

Bush vetch is one of the most common of the many meadow and scrubland vetches that occur in Wales. It is a climber, often covering the taller plants of field margins.

< 18mm >

Common vetch *(Vicia sativa)* has a slightly shorter blooming season - typically late May to mid September - and is distinguished from bush vetch by its pinker flowers with much paler wings. Originating from mainland Europe and used as a source of seeds for feeding pigeons, common vetch is another grassland and field margin wildflower of the pea family, Fabaceae. (The Latin family name is applied specifically to broad beans, *Vicia faba*.)

Bumblebees find bush vetch and common vetch particularly attractive because of the nectar that their flowers provide.

Jan   Feb   Mar   Apr   May   Jun   Jul   Aug   Sep   Oct   Nov   Dec

White Clover *(Trifolium repens)*

< **25mm** >

White clover (also known as Dutch clover) is widespread throughout Wales. The scented flowers are a rather dull white, sometimes with a pinkish tinge; bees love them.

The generic name *Trifolium* is a reference to the trefoil leaves, but if you search thoroughly you may be lucky enough to find a four-leaved clover. The specific name *repens* refers to the creeping stems that take root as they progress along the ground, making this a difficult weed to eradicate.

46   Jan   Feb   Mar   Apr   May   Jun   Jul   Aug   Sep   Oct   Nov   Dec

Red Clover *(Trifolium Pratense)*

20mm

The most common of our pink/purple clovers, this species is grown as a fodder crop or for ploughing in as a nitrogen-rich fertiliser. Bacteria in the root systems of red clover 'fix' nitrogen from the air, turning it into salts that other plants can make use of.

In some country areas red clover flowers are still used to make a potent wine; and in the past it was used as the basis of a sweet syrup treatment for whooping cough.

Clover is mainly pollinated by bumblebees, and beekeepers sometimes place hives beside clover fields so that their bees can collect the nectar. As a result red clover is also known as bee bread.

All clover species are members of the pea family, Fabaceae.

Jan   Feb   Mar   Apr   May   Jun   Jul   Aug   Sep   Oct   Nov   Dec   *47*

Autumn Hawkbit *(Leontodon autumnalis)*

< 25mm >

A perennial member of the Asteraceae, autumn hawkbit is sometimes mistaken for a dandelion, although its flower stalks are never hollow like those of dandelions. (Rather more like a dandelion is **catsear *(Hypochoeris radicata)*** another hawkbit, but its leaves and stems are covered in fine hairs rather than being smooth like those of a dandelion.)

Autumn hawkbit petals are squared at the tips. The flowers close up when pollinated and open again to release the seeds on downy carriers, but the seed heads remain cup shaped rather than forming a full sphere like those of dandelions (see page 15).

This common wildflower does for dry meadows in autumn what the common dandelion does for pastures across Wales in springtime: it creates wonderful swathes of gold.

Jan   Feb   Mar   Apr   May   Jun   Jul   Aug   Sep   Oct   Nov   Dec

Clustered Bellflower *(Campanula glomerata)*

< 25mm >

The Latin names *Campanula* (which means little bell) and *glomerata* (in clusters) perfectly describe the form of this charming wildflower. Clustered bellflower needs rich chalk-based grassland, and one of the very few remaining sites in Wales for this species is at Kenfig National Nature Reserve. It has also been reported from the Denbighshire-Flintshire area.

Jan   Feb   Mar   Apr   May   Jun   Jul   Aug   Sep   Oct   Nov   Dec   *49*

Dropwort *(Filipendula vulgaris)*

< 10mm >

Dropwort is a member of the rose family, Rosaceae. Easily mistaken for its close relative Meadowsweet (*Filipendula ulmaria* – see page 51), dropwort usually favours fast-draining near-neutral or alkaline soil. It can be found in most limestone heath areas including the Great Orme's Head in North Wales and Gower Commons in South Wales.

The featherlike leaves are edible when young, and in the past the root tubers were also considered a useful if somewhat inferior vegetable. The generic name *Filipendula* comes from the Greek words *filum*, meaning a thread, and *pendulus*, meaning hanging. The tubers of this plant are indeed attached to the roots by thin thread-like structures. The specific name *vulgaris* means common, although this wildflower is nowhere near as common in Wales as it is in other parts of the British Isles. Birds, bees, butterflies and beetles are attracted to the scentless flowers, just two of whose claimed medicinal values were as treatments for chest ailments and for kidney complaints.

Meadowsweet *(Filipendula ulmaria)*

< 6mm >

iny, scented cream flowers in tighter clusters than those of dropwort help to identify eadowsweet, a herb containing salicylic acid (the basis of aspirin). Although taken on its wn salicylic acid (and indeed aspirin) can cause internal bleeding, the tannin and mucilage meadowsweet are reputed to help protect the stomach. As a result this plant has a long story of use in herbal medicine. Meadowsweet occurs in damp grassland throughout ales and makes an attractive show in field borders and beside some ponds and streams.

Jan Feb Mar Apr May Jun Jul Aug Sep Oct Nov Dec *51*

Tall Ramping Fumitory *(Fumaria bastardii)*

Plants of arable land, despite lacking tendrils the various fumitories climb over corn and other crops. The hermaphrodite flowers (having male and female organs) are self-fertile.

25mm

At least four other fumitory species occur in Wales, including **white ramping fumitory (*Fumaria capreolata*)**, pictured on the left.

Fumitory seeds are long-lived and can germinate if a field is disturbed after many years of lying fallow.

The fumitory family, Fumariaceae, also includes various *Corydalis* species as well as **bleeding heart (*Dicentra formosa*)**, all of which have become naturalised in many parts of Wales.

Common Valerian *(Valeriana officinalis)*

< 5mm >

A tall perennial plant of grassland, common valerian is found in damp meadows throughout Wales. The very pale pink flowers open from much darker pink buds.

There is something in the scent of common valerian that makes it particularly attractive to cats. Allegedly rats also find the dried roots alluring - so much so that in the past valerian roots were used in traps set to capture rodents.

Valerian is not generally used as a food. It has, however, been used as a mild sedative in the treatment of nervous disorders. Despite several reports of poisoning when consumed in large doses, this wildflower has inexplicably acquired the alternative common name of all-heal.

The generic name may refer to an early herbalist named Valerian, who promoted its virtues. An alternative origin might be the Latin *valere* meaning to be in good health. The specific name *officinalis* was given to plants deemed to have medical value.

Meadow Saxifrage *(Saxifraga granulata)*

Of all the saxifrages that grow in Wales, meadow saxifrage has the largest flowers. Favouring lime-based grassland, this wildflower was once widespread throughout the Principality, but the destruction of its preferred habitat has made it much less common. In Roman times meadow saxifrage was used in herbal treatments for gallstones.

< 25mm >

The name saxifrage means stone-breaking and comes from its frequent occurrence in rocky crevices and the (false) assumption that the plant had literally broken through the rock.

In the traditional nursery rhyme about Mary's garden, the 'pretty maids all in a row' may be a reference to the garden variety of *Saxifraga granulata. H*owever, given the satirical nature of such verses a more sinister explanation is at least as likely. In this the 'pretty maids' are rows of guillotines erected on the orders of the English queen Mary Tudor. (The only gardens they filled were graveyards!)

Common Bistort *(Persicaria bistorta)*

Common bistort can create the most spectacular summer displays in damp meadows. This perennial, which often grows to almost a metre in height, is found in most parts of Wales.

The Latin specific name *bistorta* means twice twisted, a reference to the snaking underground stems that are also the origin of its alternative common names of snakeweed and adderwort.

In Wales as elsewhere, young leaves of common bistort have long been a popular salad vegetable. In parts of northern England bistort is a key ingredient of Eastertide dishes known as dock pudding and Easter-ledge pudding. The heart-shaped leaves are mixed with other chopped leaves such as nettle and dandelion, to which are added oatmeal, pearl barley, butter, eggs, onions, salt and pepper; then the whole lot is either fried or boiled in a muslin bag. The fine details of the recipes are jealously guarded in Yorkshire, where a dock pudding competition is held annually in the village of Mytholmroyd.

Bistort is a member of the knotweed and dock family, the Polygonaceae.

< 15mm >

Jan   Feb   Mar   Apr   May   Jun   Jul   Aug   Sep   Oct   Nov   Dec

Corn Sow-thistle *(Sonchus arvensis)*

45mm

Found throughout lowland Wales, the corn sow-thistle, also commonly referred to as field milk-thistle, grows to well over a metre in height. It is a perennial weed of arable land, although modern herbicides have reduced its occurrence in crop fields. You will also find this plant on limestone grassland and neutral heaths, but it is much less common in areas where the soil is strongly acidic. The yellowish sticky hairs on the flower bracts distinguish this member of the family Asteraceae from **smooth sow-thistle *(Sonchus oleraceus)*** and **rough sow-thistle *(Sonchus asper)*** both of which are common on disturbed wasteland and field margins in Wales.

Because their stems exude a milky latex when they are broken, sow-thistles were fed to lactating sows in the belief that milk production would increase – hence the common name.

Yellow Pimpernel *(Lysimachia nemorum)*

< 12mm >

The lovely star-like flowers of yellow pimpernel open out flat in sunny weather and close during rain or when there is heavy cloud cover. It is a wildflower of damp grassland and field edges but, as the specific name *nemorum* implies, yellow pimpernel also occurs in woodland clearings.

Although the common name might suggest a close relationship with **scarlet pimpernel, Anagallis arvensis**, the *Lysimachia* generic name places it botanically with some of the loosestrifes – for example **yellow loosestrife, Lysimachia vulgaris**.

< 20mm >

Creeping Jenny, Lysimachia nummularia (the specific name means 'round and flat like a coin' – a reference to the leaf shape) is similar in habitat needs and growing habit to yellow pimpernel. Its flowers are much larger and open only into a cup shape rather than flattening out completely.

In the past, the leaves of this perennial were used as a wound dressing. The leaves and flowers are still used today to make a kind of tea.

Now a popular garden plant, this member of the primrose family (Primulaceae) is uncommon in Wales and absent from much of Gwynedd.

Jan   Feb   Mar   Apr   May   Jun   Jul   Aug   Sep   Oct   Nov   Dec   *57*

Common Broom *(Cytisus scoparius)*

Broom, a member of the pea family, Fabaceae, has tiny deciduous leaves. Because its stalks are bright green, it can create the false impression that it is an evergreen shrub.

Broom is most common on heaths, where the **mountain pansy, *Viola lutea*** (left), was once plentiful throughout Wales. The mountain pansy's range has been contracting in recent times, but these variable blue, yellow or yellow-and-blue wildflowers can still be found in fair numbers in parts of Snowdonia, while occasional colonies remain in the Cambrian Mountains and in the Brecon Beacons.

Mountain pansies are distinguished from other common wild pansies – for example *Viola tricolor* var *curtisii*, found on sand dunes – by their larger size and their relatively short sepals.

All pansies belong to the violet family, Violaceae.

Common Sorrel *(Rumex acetosa)*

The leaves of common sorrel have a vinegary taste, due to the presence of oxalic acid, and so in the past this common grassland plant was used as flavouring much as lemons are nowadays. (The specific name comes from the Latin *acetum*, meaning vinegar.) Common sorrel is found in some mountain areas as well as in lowland meadows throughout Wales.

> 6mm <

Chopped sorrel leaves have been added to sauces for serving with fish. Another former use for this plant was as a rust stain remover: sap from the crushed leaves was rubbed into a stained area of cloth and the acid drew out the stains.

In late summer as the seeds (shown left) ripen they turn a beautiful shade of red, and in dry weather the leaves also blush and brighten the hay meadows.

Common sorrel is a member of the dock family, Polygonaceae.

Lesser Burdock *(Arctium minus)*

< 20mm >

Also called sticky buttons, lesser burdock is common on dry scrubland throughout Wales.

The name burdock comes from the hooked seed covers, or burrs, and dock, an Old English word for plant. When children pick and throw the seed heads, the hooks stick on to the clothing of their target victim.

When in 1941 the Swiss inventor George de Mestral walked his dog through a meadow containing burdock plants, the flower heads became entangled in the dog's long fur. For the next ten years de Mestral studied the clinging capability of burdock hooks and experimented with synthetic equivalents until, in 1951, he was able to patent the outstandingly successful Velcro^{TM} fastening system of interlocking nylon hooks and loops.

Greater burdock (*Arctium lappa*), a somewhat sturdier plant, has more rounded leaves and larger flower heads on longer stalks.

Burdocks belong to the daisy family, Asteracea

Musk Thistle *(Carduus nutans)*

< 50mm >

Of all the thistles that grace our grasslands the beautiful musk thistle, with fine web-like threads around its bracts, must rank as the queen. Its nodding heads are unmistakable.

Musk thistles are tall (typically growing to a metre and occasionally more) lime-loving plants that occur everywhere in Wales except for the most acidic upland areas. Spiny leaves together with sharp spines along the winged stems make this a sheep-proof plant.

Spear thistle, *Cirsium vulgare* (left), is another prickly grassland species found throughout Wales. Growing to a height of 1.5 metres, this stately wildflower is much loved by butterflies - notably the painted lady (*Vanessa cardui*) – and, when the seeds ripen, by birds such as goldfinches. Farmers, on the other hand, are less enamoured by this prickly biennial plant which, under the Weed Act, is listed as an 'injurious weed'.

Thistles belong to the Asteraceae, the daisy family (also commonly cited as Compositae).

Perforate St John's Wort *(Hypericum perforatum)*

Because it prefers alkaline or at least neutral soils, perforate St John's wort is most commonly seen in Wales on heathland on or near the limestone rich coastal strip.

Still very much in demand today as a herbal remedy, in the past this plant was used to treat the wounds of battle. Tiny see-through patches in the leaves were thought to signify that the plant had the ability to repair holes in itself and by analogy (in an ancient belief known as the 'doctrine of signatures') also in people.

Trailing St John's wort, *Hypericum humifusum* (left) is another common find in Wales; it occurs in dry acid heathland.

The St John's wort family is known as Clusiaceae.

Common Mallow *(Malva sylvestris)*

< 35mm >

Of the many kinds of mallow to be seen in Wales common mallow is the most abundant and widespread. This plant thrives on waste ground and copes well with drought conditions.

< 50mm >

Common mallow is usually a solitary plant, but on disturbed field margins it can occasionally provide a most impressive blanket cover.

Musk mallow *(Malva moschata)* is distinguished by its finely dissected upper leaves (see left); the basal leaves are rounded and three-lobed, rather like those of common mallow.

In Morocco, as in several other countries in northern Africa, mallow leaves are eaten as an alternative to spinach. They have also been used in herbal remedies, and in the past some herbalists have promoted mallow as an effective laxative.

The mallow family, Malvaceae, contains more than 1000 species, most originating in South America. Many of these, including hibiscus and hollyhock, are grown in gardens and occasionally can be seen in the wild, usually near towns or villages.

Bramble *(Rubus fruticosus)*

< 20mm >

From August to the end of October, blackberry pickers (avian and human) descend on heaths and hedgerows all \over Wales to gather the delicious fruity berries of brambles. The pale pink or white flowers can be seen in spring, summer and autumn.

Other members of the *Rubus* genus to be found in Wales include the **wild raspberry *(Rubus idaeus)*** and the (now quite rare) **cloudberry (*Rubus chamaemorus*)**. Cloudberries (left) are unusual in having fruits that are bright orange when fully ripe. These alpine 'blackberries' can be found in the Berwyn mountains to the south of the Dee Valley.